A Letter from Your Teacher
on the last day of School

Written by
Shannon Olsen

Illustrated by
Sandie Sonke

ISBN - Paperback: 9781735414140 Hardcover: 9781735414157 Mini book: 979-8-9874080-6-3

Library of Congress Number - 2021922951

Copyright © Shannon Olsen, Life Between Summers
Illustrations © Sandie Sonke
Printed 2024 - All Rights Reserved
lifebetweensummers.com

No part of this publication may be reproduced, distributed, or transmitted in any form
or by any means, including photocopying, recording, or other electronic or mechanical
methods unless granted written permission from the copyright holder.

For every teacher who has had to say good-bye to a special class. -S.O.

For Mom and Dad. -S.S.

Dear Student,

How are you? It's me again!
As your teacher and your friend,
I just can't believe this school year
is now coming to an end.

Can you think way back
to our first day of school?
You might have felt unsure,
meeting new friends and learning rules.

But it did not take long
for all of us to discover
that our class was something special
and unlike any other.

We grew to be a family,

as you all learned and made mistakes.

You've laughed a lot together too.

We needed those brain breaks!

You added and subtracted
and practiced strategies in math.

When given a word problem,
you worked to find a path.

We asked questions during reading
and answered quite a few.
You wrote sentences with capitals,
ending with punctuation too.

We had fun events this year

and many holidays, no less.

You smiled big on Picture Day

SAY Cheese!

and we can't forget recess!

Days weren't always perfect.
Some work was even tough.

But every time you tried your best,
that was always good enough.

Not only am I proud of all the hard work you have done,

but you've also made good choices
and I know you've only just begun.

It might feel sad to say good-bye.
Change can be hard for everyone.

But you're ready for new challenges

and a summer full of fun!

As you start a brand new grade,
I have no doubt you'll be a star.
Your new teacher will soon learn
just how wonderful you are!

Stop by and visit me in future years,
wherever you are coming from.

I'd love to hear how you are doing
and see how tall you have become.

♡ Fareu

We'll always have our memories
even when this year is through.
You've become a special part of me,
and our class is now a part of you.

Love,

_____

Dear Teacher,

If you happened to read my letter to you at the end of *A Letter From Your Teacher: On the First Day of School,* well then...hello, it's me again! I am guessing a lot has happened between the beginning of the school year and now.

The school year goes through a lot of phases, doesn't it? The first day has that shiny and new feeling, right down to the school supplies. From there, things seem to get rolling right into a whirlwind. You get up to your ears in lesson planning, grading, and staff meetings that could have been an email. Soon it's pumpkin everything, then a winter holiday flurry, and before you know it, teachers start feeling the spring fever just as much as their students.

In those final weeks leading up to the last day of school, most teachers are especially TIRED. Long gone is that shiny and new feeling from back to school time. You have worked incredibly hard all year, and may be counting down the days to summer vacation.

But the end of the year is also bittersweet. In the midst of all those busy day-to-day routines, you ended up building this little family with your students. All of you have a sense of comfort and familiarity with one another. You've been there to witness your class' struggles, their proud moments, and their growth over many months.

And you have gotten to know your kids in a way that only their teacher can. You're in tune with each of their personalities. You know all the tried and true "tricks" to help support their individual learning styles. You're aware of who might be going through a big change at home, like a new baby sibling or a parents' divorce. You genuinely care about them as people.

On the first day of school, you had so much new information to present to them. And now on the last day, it's a different kind of message to share. You'll be giving your kids an opportunity to reflect on their memories, and how far they've come this year. You may want them to know how much you'll miss them, but how you also wish them all the best for the future.

Whenever you want to send well wishes to another adult, one way of doing that is through a greeting card. We don't always have all the words to fully verbalize our feelings (especially when it comes to good-byes). A card can help us out with communicating the sentiment we would like to get across.

When kids are the ones you are wanting to send a special message to, a picture book is like a teacher's version of a greeting card. A read aloud can help convey what some of us may not have all the words for. I wrote this book as a basis for what you might want to express to your students before they leave your classroom for the last time. My hope is that it helps your class in celebrating and reflecting on the time you've had together.

When bidding farewell to this group of kids, know that they are also going to miss YOU (no matter how excited they may be for summer vacation). Over the course of the school year, you have become their comfort zone. Your kids would probably tell a substitute, "That's not how our teacher does it." They are used to you! Your students are familiar with the phrases you say most often, and random little tidbits, like if you drink coffee. And there are many things you've instilled that will stick with them long after they've left your class.

One of the lines you will read aloud to your students on the last page of this book is, "You've become a special part of me." As one of the most important people during this time in their lives, you've become a very special part of them too.

With love,

About the Author

Shannon Olsen has taught second grade for fifteen years. She is from Southern California and obtained her B.A. in English and M.A. in Teaching from University of California, Irvine. Shannon loves traveling and spending time with her husband and two daughters. Visit www.lifebetweensummers.com for her teacher resources, book companions, and information about author visits.

About the Illustrator

Sandie Sonke is also a Southern California native with a degree in studio art from California State University Fullerton. She is a fan of coffee and cooking, and among the many hats she wears, her favorite role is being a mom of two. Sandie has published several children's books, and you can also find more of her freelance illustration work at www.sandiesonkeillustration.com.